The Ride Guide

What you don't know CAN hurt you!

Lisa Creedon

ALCOVY PRESS
WWW.ALCOVYPRESS.COM

Contents

Published by
Alcovy Press
Atlanta, Georgia
2014.3055

Special Thanks to
Jimmy Merck, Master Mechanic,
Officer Ben Muckle, Gwinnett County Police Department,
Steve Watson, Service Advisor,
and Tim Barker, Automotive Technician
for their input and technical expertise.

ISBN: 9780983303923

Library of Congress Control No.: 2012917789

Printed in the United States of America

For more information, contact www.alcovypress.com

Foreword

The Ride Guide: What you don't know CAN hurt you!
A valuable car guide for both new and experienced drivers.

When my 18 year old daughter became the victim of a "bump and grab," (page 12) we learned a lot from the police officers who answered the call. Not only did we learn how fortunate she was in not being injured or having her car stolen, we also learned how to avoid this type of danger and a whole lot more.

Since my daughter's incident, I have researched crimes that occur while driving, the crimes that don't often make it to the evening news. By being aware of our surroundings and noticing potentially suspicious circumstances, many of these crimes can be avoided. My mission is to educate others on these dangers, particularly young drivers. Much of the information in this book was based on cases of need or trouble, and real cases of specific incidents are included.

Along with warnings of potential driving dangers, *The Ride Guide* also provides loads of useful information about taking care of your car, how to talk to a police officer, how to avoid getting a ticket, accidents – what to do and how to avoid them, important driving tips, and much more!

Learn how to buy a used car, how to use jumper cables, how to avoid being stranded, when not to use cruise control, and many other valuable tips. In the back of the book, handy forms are provided for doing maintenance checks and for keeping track of vehicle service and purchases – a great tool for your personal records as well as when selling a car.

While new drivers generally have the most current driving knowledge, they don't know many of the points mentioned in this book – things learned from years of driving experience. However, drivers of any age and experience level will benefit from *The Ride Guide*. A perfect size for your glove box, this important information is always at your fingertips!

Who's Watching You?

Have you seen the news lately?! Regardless of where we live, crime rates are up. This information is not meant to scare but to help us be more informed and alert to dangers lurking around us. Once we develop safe habits, we will be more aware of our surroundings as we drive or when returning to our cars from work or shopping. We will be less likely to experience problems.

The following items may not include every situation, but these are important points to know and could possibly save your life. Teen drivers, mothers of young children, and women are more often targeted; however, anyone is at risk.

- If blue lights (or red & blue lights) are flashing behind you while driving in a rural area or isolated city area, whether at night or daytime, *do not stop* – even if you are speeding – unless you know for sure it is a real police car. Reduce your speed and turn on your hazard lights/4-way flashers (and interior light if at night) to indicate you acknowledge the blue lights – important if it really is a police officer. Drive to a populated, well-lighted area before stopping.

If possible, call 911 on your cell phone and ask if an officer is on that road attempting to stop a vehicle. They call in their activities, so the 911 operator can tell you if this is a legitimate traffic stop. If you call 911, advise them you are continuing to a populated area.

Many robberies, and worse crimes, are committed with the help of fake police-type lights installed in a car's grill, and the lights are easily purchased online. This particular crime occurs often and happens in daytime as well as at night.

Important: Unmarked police cars are not usually involved in traffic stops. If the car is using a single flashing light or if the lights are in the grill instead of on top of the car, be more cautious about stopping.

- Keep keys in your hand while walking to your car. Check the floor of your vehicle (front and back) before entering. Once inside, immediately lock your doors. *Always drive with the doors locked* and the windows up, no matter how safe you think the area might be.

- When walking through a parking lot chatting on a phone, we are less likely to notice someone watching us. This makes us an easy mark, more so if we have packages or are pushing a stroller.

To a thief, a stroller or a distracted shopper means he will not be seen approaching while a child is fastened into a car seat or packages are unloaded. Cell phone use and small children can make women an easy target.

- When leaving a bank or store, do not sit in your car counting money or looking through your wallet. If you need to count money or look for something, drive to a different location in the parking lot.

- Be more cautious in the months when it gets dark early; the crime rate increases. This is particularly true during the holiday season. Never walk to your car with cash in your hand, and never leave cash where it can be seen in your car.

Also, do not leave valuables in your car. If you cannot afford to replace an item, do not leave it in your car. Items stolen from a car are claimed on your homeowner's insurance – with that deductible.

- Hide your packages – keep an old blanket in the car if you are planning to shop at several different stores. If you take packages to your car and plan to go back inside the store or mall, move your car to a different parking place.

- When returning to your car from shopping, be aware of your surroundings. Notice if someone is sitting in the passenger side of the car parked next to yours and if they seem to be watching you. Do not make eye contact; it can give unspoken permission to speak to you.

- Be alert if a van is parked next to your car, especially a cargo van with someone sitting in the passenger seat. Cargo vans are a favorite tool for kidnapping. If you are ever grabbed, try to yell FIRE instead of HELP. Studies have shown people to be more responsive to shouts of *Fire*.

- Another option is to return to the store (or mall) and ask a manager or security guard to walk you to your car. The police can also be called to escort you to your car. Never take a chance on your safety! Better to deal with inconvenience or feeling overly cautious than for your family to be planning a funeral.

• Ever hear of Ted Bundy, the famous serial killer? He was attractive, charming and intelligent. He frequently used a cane or crutch and sometimes wore bandages, giving the appearance of an injured or disabled man in need of assistance. His victims were happy to help – and then were kidnapped and murdered. He was able to easily overpower his victims because they were not expecting a kind, handsome, disabled man to attack them.

• Do not let a stranger engage you in an odd conversation. If the person makes you feel uncomfortable, do not respond even if the request is for help or directions. A favorite ploy is to ask for help in finding something: directions, looking for a child, a lost puppy or something else that might be appealing to the selected victim.
  Be suspicious and be alert. Always trust your instincts (gut feelings). If you get a bad feeling about someone, leave immediately. Do not worry about hurting their feelings. Dangerous people are excellent con men, and they know how to play on the sympathies of others. There are also "con women." Trust your feelings and avoid situations that make you uncomfortable.

• If someone is in need of help and you choose to help, offer to make a phone call *for* them or to call 911. Never give your phone to a stranger, even for "just a quick call."

• Another favorite ploy is for the stranger to mumble something to his targeted victim. The victim, not wanting to appear rude, moves closer and asks the person to repeat what was said. Do not worry about appearing rude – beware! Moving closer to the stranger could put you within easy grabbing distance. It is best to beware of strangers.

• Once you have started your car, do not get out if you hear a noise. Drive to another place before you stop your car to check on the noise. Car thieves might have tied something to the back bumper.

Here is how that works: The driver starts his/her car, puts it in gear and begins to drive away. He then hears a noise. Without turning off the car, the driver stops and gets out of the car to look behind it. Then, very quickly, someone either jumps into the car and drives away or the driver is attacked or kidnapped.

• When traveling late at night or in a deserted area, be extra cautious. If a driver motions something is wrong with your car, do not stop your car until reaching a well-lit, populated area. Then, if you choose to interact with this person, stop your car where it is not blocked and you are prepared for a quick getaway if necessary.

• If parked in a questionable area or if your car has been unattended for an extended period of time, walk around the car to make sure tires are all inflated, doors are still locked and nothing obvious is wrong. It is best to park in lots that have an attendant. At night, try to park in well-lighted areas with pedestrian traffic.
When checking your car, also look at your trunk. Newer cars allow access into the car through the trunk, and a small hole near the trunk latch could mean the lock has been disabled. If your trunk latch has been compromised, you were likely robbed or someone could be in your trunk (or the back of your SUV) – waiting to come through the back seat area while you are driving. If you have any suspicions at all, call the police before getting into your car.

• If you think a car might be following you, do not go home. Go to an open store or gas station (that you can enter quickly) to see if the car follows you there. It is important is to get to a place where you have the safety of other people around you. If the suspicious car follows you to the "safe" place, try to get the make and model of the car, the license number if possible, and call 911.

• If you return to your car and have a flat tire, immediately go back into the store (or your workplace) to call for help. If a stranger approaches you in the parking lot and offers to fix your flat tire, unfortunately, you might be putting yourself at risk to accept that offer. The stranger could have been responsible for causing the flat tire so you would be an easy target to rob or worse. It is terrible to be so suspicious because many of us have been helped by strangers; however, take into consideration where you are, time of day, gut feelings about the stranger, etc. before allowing a stranger into your personal space.

• If you choose to carry a gun in your car, it is best to take a gun safety course to learn how to properly and effectively shoot. Also, know the requirements in your state regarding gun carrying laws.

Two more important points:
• If you are meeting a stranger for any reason – interview, selling something, first date, etc., meet that person in a busy, reputable public place. Always be cautious of letting strangers know where you live and at home, be especially careful about opening your door to a stranger. While many home invasions are forced entry, some invaders have politely knocked at the front door!

• Just as pilots file a flight plan before leaving on a trip, always make sure someone knows where you are going. If anything were to happen, it is best if the police know where to begin looking.
    Send a text message, leave a note on the kitchen counter, email a parent or friend – and encourage your friends to do that too. People disappear, especially women, and precious time is lost as police try to reconstruct the path that person took.

    Real case: A college student was driving home from school, a five hour drive. Thankfully, she called home when she was a few miles away. She never arrived home, but police knew the search area was only a few miles – not spread over a five hour drive. Still, it took awhile before a detective noticed trees that were scraped about ten feet off the ground.
    They found the student in her car down an embankment. She had left the roadway, airborne, gone through trees, and ended up in a river bank. Sadly, she had probably died on impact – only a few miles from home. Without her phone call to go on, she might have never been found.

Crimes of Convenience

Crime of Convenience is the new buzzword for the popular crime spree sweeping across the country. As we continue looking for every possible convenience to make our lives easier and faster, criminals are looking at new opportunities for easy money.

- Movie Rentals – We used to go inside a store to rent movies. Now, we have the convenience of swiping a credit card through a machine outside of a store. Daylight hours are generally safer; however, criminals are watching people who go after dark.

     When getting a movie, reserve it online if possible. That means your time at the machine will be minimal. Also, only take your credit card to the machine. Leave your purse or wallet locked in the car, and never leave your car idling.

- Convenience Stores – People continue to dash into the store for "just a second" while leaving their cars idling and unlocked. Many times, folks are in a hurry and don't notice a suspicious person watching the store for just such an opportunity.

     In a number of instances, cars have been stolen in the "just a second" time frame. Worse, it has happened with children in the car. Too often, "just a second" has cost us a LOT more time and heartache.

- Purses in the car – Most women do not leave their purses in the car where other people can see them. However, if the area is being watched, the criminal also knows if you leave the car *without* a purse. Moms who leave their purse in the car while they run inside the preschool to pick up their child have returned to a smashed window and no purse. The same is true at other businesses and also at parks.

     Be careful what you leave in the car. We never know who might be watching us – watching for the opportunity to steal a wallet, camera, laptop computer, and more. If you must leave something of value in your car, make sure it is covered with a towel or blanket to give you some bit of protection.

- ATM Crime – ATM crime is also on the rise. Especially at night, before using the ATM, look around for anything that might seem suspicious – a vehicle parked oddly, people sitting in cars. If you have any bad feelings about the situation, leave quickly. There have been numerous incidents where people have received cash from the ATM, only to have a thief run up and grab the cash and bank card.

Overall, it is best to avoid outside transactions at night or in areas that are not well-lighted or visible to passing motorists. If you must go out, take a friend with you. However, that in itself is not total protection. Criminals often work in pairs too.

- Recently, a new crime wave is sweeping the U.S. Thieves are breaking into cars to obtain addresses and garage door openers. The victim does not even know anything is wrong until he gets home and does not have a garage door opener.

While the unsuspecting victims are at work, church, the movies, school events, sporting events, etc., thieves quickly use a "Slim Jim" to open/jimmy the car door, grab the garage door opener, and locate the owner's address from information in the glove box. It only takes a few seconds. The thieves then drive to the victim's house, use the garage door opener to park in the garage, close the garage door, and know they have hours to peacefully rob the house.

Most of us keep our insurance and vehicle registration cards, both of which may show our full name and home address, in an unlocked glove box. However, people with the right tools to break into a vehicle would likely have no problem popping open a locked glove box.

When you leave your car for a length of time, take your garage door opener with you. At a minimum, make sure your door opener is well hidden.

Avoiding a Bad Situation

Your most important decision is to avoid a potentially bad situation. By paying attention to your surroundings and planning ahead, your travels can be safer. Some basic tips include:

- Get gas during daylight hours at a safe location.
- Learn alternate routes to your destination; your GPS is not programmed to avoid bad areas. This is also true (and important) when traveling to unfamiliar cities/states.
- Make sure car doors are locked and windows are up at all times, regardless how safe the area might seem. If you need fresh air, only open windows two inches.
- If a suspicious-looking person approaches your car, drive away immediately.
- Don't pull up too close to the car in front. Leave room to maneuver around it if the need arises. You might need to leave in a hurry.
- When in a new or suspicious area, drive in the inside or center lane to make it more difficult for potential carjackers to target your car.
- Do not stop to assist a stranger whose car appears to have broken down. The car might not be broken down (just a ploy to get someone to stop) or the stopped car might not even belong to the person standing beside it. Call 911 to report that someone has a problem.
- Keep your car in good repair to reduce the possibility of a breakdown. If your car quits, stay inside and call someone – a friend, 511 or 911. Do not start walking down the road.
- Call 911 if you believe you are in, or think you are about to experience, a bad situation. There might be a nearby police car that could save your life.

If You Are Grabbed

• Never willingly get into someone else's car. Once you are in the car, your chances for survival diminish greatly. Kick, scream, and fight with everything you have to avoid being taken (keys can be a weapon) and grab anything you can: street sign, lamp post, trash can, etc. If you are too much trouble or attract too much attention, he may let you go.

• Yell "FIRE" instead of Help to attract attention. Studies have shown that people respond more quickly to shouts of fire. However, screams of "I'm being kidnapped" should also encourage onlookers to call the police.

• Hide your cell phone. If your phone is not grabbed immediately, hide it and call 911 at the first opportunity.

• If you are put in a trunk, try to kick out a tail light or find something in the trunk that could be used to break the tail light. Also feel around for a weapon – a lug wrench (for removing tire bolts) could be in there. Once there is an opening through the tail light area, wave something – your hand, a piece of clothing, etc. out the opening. People have done this and been saved by an alert driver following that car.

Real case: A girl was grabbed and thrown into the back seat of a car. She dialed 911 and let them hear what was happening. She helped the police find her by identifying locations they were passing without letting her kidnappers know. She was yelling things like, "Where are you taking me in this black car? Alley Street, now Adams Street? Are we going toward town?" Her quick thinking probably saved her life.

If You Have an Accident

When involved in a car accident, call 911 immediately. Your insurance company will ask if there is a police report. Sometimes injuries can show up later (especially neck or back problems). Once the information is recorded, it is easier to file medical claims. Also, if there is no police report and the other party decides not to pay for the damage to your car or does not report the accident to his insurance company, you have no recourse.

Witnesses are useful if they actually saw the accident happen, not if they noticed after hearing the impact. However, they could testify to aggressive driving behavior, cell phone use, etc. prior to the accident.

When involved in an accident, do not say it was your fault, whether you think it was or not. Newest info says you should not even say "I'm sorry" because that could be used as an admission of guilt if the other driver decides to sue.

It is best not to talk about the accident except to the police officer. In some situations, an accident can appear to be the fault of one driver but on closer examination, a decision by the other driver could have been the real cause.

Exchange information with the other driver: name, address, phone number, insurance company name and policy number, license tag number and the VIN (vehicle identification number) of the car.

Moving Damaged Vehicles

If the accident is blocking the roadway or an intersection, the cars should be moved if drivable and if there are no injuries. Take pictures of the accident with your cell phone before moving the cars.

If There Are Injuries

Call 911 for emergency services, then try to help the person as much as possible. Do not move or lift them unless it is absolutely necessary. If they must be moved, try to keep them in the same position in which they were found. This is done to prevent further injury. Stop serious bleeding with thick cloths, as clean as possible, and apply pressure by hand. Keep the person warm. In cold weather, if possible, cover the person with blankets or coats.

Know the law in your state regarding care for injuries in a vehicle accident. Some states have a *Good Samaritan Law*, which holds the caregiver harmless from lawsuits that could result from problems in administering emergency care.

Accidents on Private Property

On private property, like a mall or shopping center parking lot, you should still call the police. Depending on the circumstances, they might not be able to write a ticket, but the report could be useful for filing an insurance claim. Particularly if there are injuries or other complications (such as a DUI), it is best to have a police report.

Accidents with Suspicious Circumstances

When another car hits our car from behind, we generally stop and get out of the car to assess the damage. When is this a bad idea?

If involved in an accident while driving in a questionable or isolated area, especially at night – *or if you are suspicious of the circumstances*, do not get out of your car and do not turn off your car. If a car hits yours or stops quickly causing you to hit that car, it could be a scam where you might be mugged or carjacked *(also known as a "bump & grab" – see story on page 12)*.

Leave. Use your hazard lights/4-way flashers and motion to the other driver to follow so you will not be accused of a hit and run. If the other driver does not follow you, try to get the license plate number and make/color of that car. Call 911 to report the incident and advise you are driving to a safer location. Many times there is no actual damage to the victim's car.

Drive to the nearest populated, well-lighted (if at night) place you feel is safe before stopping to check the damage and talk to the other driver (if he followed you). It is best to meet inside the store. You might want to wait for the police to arrive before getting out of your car.

If you do not have a cell phone to call 911, do not get out of your car. Drive to the nearest well-lighted, populated place and call 911 from there.

Real Case: An 18 year old girl ("Ann") was working at a stadium in downtown Atlanta. This particular evening, the game ended late and when she left the stadium, the usual (safe) route to the expressway was closed. Using the GPS on her phone, she started through side streets, not realizing she was in one of Atlanta's more dangerous neighborhoods.

When her car was bumped from behind, she stopped and got out to look for damage. The elderly woman driver was mumbling senselessly and the irate younger passenger scared Ann, so she turned around – only to find a large gang gathered around her. Her days-old smart phone was quickly snatched from her hand, and the thugs started moving in closer and touching her. For those who believe in divine intervention, this was it. A taller man moved toward her and the gang stepped back. The man was frightening in appearance but told Ann to get back in her car, lock the doors and leave. The gang seemed to melt into the night.

Traumatized, she sat there crying, and a young woman appeared at the car window. She said she had watched everything from her house and offered to call the police. She also offered a place to stay while waiting for the police to arrive and to lock the car in their garage so it would not be harmed. Ann used the girl's phone to call her mom with all the information, and Ann accepted the girl's invitation.

The police arrived 1½ hours later – not surprising for that area of town because no one was injured and the police had numerous, more serious calls that took precedence over this one. One of the officers told Ann the proper procedure in this type situation (which preceded this story), then said he couldn't believe the gang didn't hurt her or steal her car. She quit her job the next day.

Every city has areas that are less safe. Your GPS does not know that information. New drivers and people new to the city should learn where those areas are located. Ask people which areas to avoid, and use a map to learn alternate routes when traveling outside of familiar territory.

Travelers have been robbed and worse when driving in unfamiliar cities. Learn about where you are going before you go!

Other Staged Accidents

While it may not happen as frequently, it is worth mentioning that there are people who intentionally cause accidents. The accidents are staged to make you at fault. Most often, these drivers plan the accident where witnesses are not around or are less likely to stop. Again, it is important to be cautious, alert, and always keep a good distance between your car and the car in front of you.

• **Rear-End Accident:** The driver will quickly pull in front of the targeted car and slam on his brakes, or simply just suddenly brake. This causes the innocent driver to rear-end the scam driver. Along with collecting money for car damage, the scam driver usually fakes medical injuries to collect even more money.

Call 911 and don't get out of your car until the police arrive. Make pictures through the windshield of the accident, including the car tag.

• **Scam-Waving:** The scam driver waves you to go in front of him, then crashes into you. He will deny waving you in when the police get there to file the report. Always be cautious, and be prepared to stop quickly if you see any movement from the other vehicle.

Fear After an Accident

After an accident, it is totally normal to feel some fear or apprehension about driving. Your confidence will return but if you are having real anxiety about driving, start out with short trips – close to home, not in prime traffic times, not on the expressway. Once you are feeling more confident, drive for longer times and work your way up to where you feel comfortable driving again.

Avoiding Accidents

How do your driving skills rate on the *Most Common Causes* list below?

The Most Common Causes of Accidents

- Tailgating – driving too close to the car in front of you
- Weather – driving too fast for conditions in rain, fog, snow, ice or high winds
- Aggressive or reckless driving, road rage
- Driving under the influence of alcohol, legal or illegal drugs
- Distracted driving – could involve cell phones, loud music, noisy passengers, eating, or looking for something in your car
- Drowsy driving – tired drivers can be as dangerous as those driving under the influence of alcohol or drugs
- Running red lights and stop signs
- Unsafe lane changes, ignoring blind spots
- Night driving – slow down when you cannot see well
- Animal crossings, particularly on rural roads

Basically, accidents happen because drivers are not paying enough attention to what they are doing.

> *The majority of accidents are caused by drivers who are speeding and/or following too close.*

While everyone knows the basics of avoiding accidents, a few reminders might be helpful:

- **Use the shoulder** – When on a two lane road or the outside lane of a highway and the driver ahead of you suddenly slams on the brakes, aim for the shoulder of the road instead of running into the back of that car. Even if you run off the road and end up needing a tow, it is MUCH better than having an insurance claim or possibly totaling your car.

• **Give yourself plenty of room to stop** – When brake lights are visible ahead, start slowing down *THEN.* Do not wait until you get closer; it is too easy to misjudge your stopping distance.

• **Following too close** – For every ten miles of speed, keep one car length's distance between you and the car in front. For example, when traveling at 40mph, there should be room for four cars to get in between you and the car in front of you. Yes, this can be more difficult on the expressway, but you must reach a point where you are more concerned with safety – for yourself as well as for other drivers – than trying to possibly reach your destination a few minutes sooner.

Watch brake lights ahead, not just the car in front but as far ahead as you can see. The driver in front of you might not be paying attention and could suddenly slam on his brakes. Do not depend on that driver to keep you alerted to problems.

• **Erratic driving** – On the expressway, if the driver ahead of you is having trouble staying in his lane, pass him and stay away from him. He may be texting, intoxicated, or falling asleep.

If a speeding driver is whipping in and out of lanes, slow down and let him get ahead of you. That type of driver is more likely to cause an accident.

• **Use your mirrors and turn your head** – When changing lanes, use your mirrors but always look over your shoulder if you have any doubt about where the other cars are. Every vehicle has blind spots.

• **Don't follow big trucks – or vehicles carrying loads** – The tires on big trucks can throw rocks at your windshield. Vehicles carrying loads can be hazardous because sometimes things are not properly tied down. There have been a number of severe injuries and deaths from ladders that were not properly secured, when the driver slammed on his brakes and sent the ladder flying into the windshield of the following car.

• **When turning left** – Look left, then right, and then left again.

- **When there are no brake lights** – If the car in front of you has no brake lights or has only one brake light, it can impair your ability to stop. If on the expressway, change lanes. On surface streets, pull into a side street if you need to; it is too easy to rear-end a car without brake lights. Through years of driving, our brains have been programmed to respond to brake lights. Even though we know to pay attention to the traffic ahead, we are more tuned in to the car directly in front of us.

- **Turn at the light if possible** – On multi-lane roads, if you have the choice, turn at a light instead of hoping all lanes of traffic will stop to let you turn. Many vehicles have been hit (T-boned) as the driver tries to cross lanes of stopped cars. The lane farthest away has less visibility and that car may not see you until it is too late to stop.

Whether or not the accident is your fault, repairing or replacing your car after an accident is inconvenient and can be expensive. Insurance deductibles are frequently $1000 or higher, and a new/used car search is usually time consuming and frustrating. When the accident is your fault, points go against your license, and too many claims can cause the insurance company to cancel your policy. When an insurance company cancels a policy, you are forced to buy insurance from a "high risk" company – which translates into "high dollars" for your insurance.

We cannot always avoid having an accident, but too many accidents happen because the driver is just not paying enough attention to driving!

> If you are already running late, an accident will not help you reach your destination more quickly!

Real case: The lady was in a hurry to get home with her three year old daughter. Traffic was not particularly heavy, and she had made this turn a hundred times before – a left turn across traffic. We all do it – decide if there is enough time to safely make the turn. She decided to take the chance, and she still visits her daughter at the graveyard, now 25 years later. If there is *any* doubt in your mind, choose to wait until you *know* you can make the turn safely.

Special Weather Circumstances

Water Hazard

Some areas of the U.S. are more likely to have flooding, but water hazards can happen anywhere. Many drivers get into trouble by trying to cross a flooded road, not knowing that the tremendous pressure and power of the water has washed away a section of the road.

Six inches of rapidly moving water can knock you off of your feet and carry you with the current. Two feet of water can float a car or bus.

Your best defense is not to drive through an area that could have unseen problems beneath the water. However, if you find yourself in a situation where your car is sinking, experts suggest the following procedure:

- Stay calm and try to think about what you should do. Do not panic. Panic may cause you to make bad decisions.
- Do not call 911 until you are out of the vehicle. You generally have less than one minute to get out. A 911 call wastes precious time, and they cannot arrive soon enough to help you. Your goal is to exit through your window as quickly as possible.
- *Most important:* As soon as you realize there is a problem, release your seat belt and roll down the window(s) before the water shorts out the electrical system. Once the car is in water, doors will not open until the car is fully submerged.
- If there are children in the car, experts suggest unstrapping the oldest child first and the youngest child last. If you have a baby, carry the child out in your arms.
- Window-breaking tools can be a lifesaver; however, keep the tool in a very accessible spot in your car.

If you do not get out before the car is fully submerged, the doors can be opened once the vehicle is full of water. However, this takes a lot of strength and unless you are able to hold your breath for a long time, you might not make it to the surface.

Snow & Ice

Those who live in parts of the country where snow and ice are just a part of winter are likely familiar with these points. In the South, however, where ice is more prevalent than snow and only occurs every few years, driving in these weather conditions is more of a challenge. Here are some pointers:

- Do not use cruise control.
- Drive slowly and leave a lot of space between your vehicle and others. It takes a lot longer to stop or turn on snow or icy roads.
- Try not to stop. Drive slowly enough to roll through a traffic light if you can. Once you stop, it is more difficult to get going again, and you risk wheel spinning.
- Accelerating can cause wheel spinning, even when going up hills. Gradually increase your speed as you approach a hill and let that carry you to the top. Reduce your speed (take foot off of accelerator) as you reach the top of the hill so you will be able to go down the hill as slowly as possible.
- Do not use your parking brake if possible. It can freeze.
- Make sure your exhaust pipe does not become clogged with snow, ice, or mud. If the exhaust pipe becomes blocked, it can send carbon monoxide gas into the vehicle. This can be fatal. And this is why you also do not warm up a vehicle in an enclosed area, like a garage.
- Clean off all windows, not just enough to see. If you do not have a scraper, a credit card will work.
- Never use hot water to defrost a window or windshield. The glass can shatter. Some people say lukewarm (barely warm) water will work.
- Especially if you live in an area prone to freezing, keep a de-icer product on hand.
- Gas lines in your vehicle can freeze. Make sure you have at least half a tank.
- Don't drive if it is not absolutely necessary.

Before the Storm: For winter driving, always be prepared. If snow or ice storms are in the forecast, keep your gas tank full. Make sure your tires have enough air (valve stems can freeze), that your radiator is full and has enough antifreeze, and that your windshield washer solvent is full. If you need an oil change, get one so your oil is full and clean. Make a grocery list and stock your pantry so you will not have to drive. Include candles, batteries, and water. Emergency Road Kits to keep in your vehicle can be purchased or you can make your own.

Emergency Road Kit: An emergency road kit for winter should include items such as:
- Drinking water
- Packaged snacks that will not go bad
- Blankets, hat, and extra clothing that is warm (for layering)
- First-Aid Supplies – if kit, make sure it contains gauze and tape
- Roll of Paper Towels
- Flashlight and extra batteries
- Cell phone car charger
- Jumper cables (don't buy the cheapest kind)
- Bag of non-clumping kitty litter to use for traction
- Shovel
- Basic tool kit

If weather forecasters say a winter storm "might hit today," realize there is a possibility the storm could come through earlier than anticipated. Especially in southern states where snow or ice storms are rare and can quickly paralyze a city, being prepared for bad road conditions can make a big difference.

In the winter of 2014, the cities of Atlanta, Georgia and Raleigh, North Carolina were brought to a stand-still by ice and snow. Drivers were trapped in their vehicles, some up to 16 hours. Having a full tank of gas made it possible for some to run their cars to stay warm while others were out of gas and suffering in the freezing cold.

When there is a possibility of a big storm, plan ahead. Before you leave for work that morning, pack a small bag with a toothbrush, toothpaste, soap, hand towel, any medications you might need, extra shoes, warm socks, snacks, and water – in addition to the Emergency Road Kit already in your car. It is better to be over-prepared and not need it than to want it and not have it!

Aggressive Driving

Most people are familiar with the terms road rage and aggressive driving but do not realize the difference. Road rage involves deliberate use of a vehicle as a weapon with intent to do harm. It is considered a physical assault to purposely harm a person or a vehicle through a traffic incident. Road rage is a criminal offense, and you can go to jail.

Aggressive driving, while regarded as less severe, can just as easily cause a serious or fatal accident. The NHTSA (National Highway Traffic Safety Administration) includes running red lights as one of the most dangerous forms of aggressive driving.

What Makes Drivers Angry

- Not using a blinker – changing lanes without notice, frequently causing other drivers to slam on brakes, usually don't make sure there is enough space to safely change lanes
- Cell Phone Users – drive slower than other traffic (usually in the "fast" lane), rarely use blinkers, cannot remember who should go next at four way stops, dangerous because they are not giving their full attention to driving a 2,000+ lb. vehicle
- Slow Drivers – everyone is in a hurry, but we must realize there are elderly drivers AND new drivers who may not feel safe driving the posted speed limit or making a left turn into heavy traffic
- Drivers who pull out in front of other vehicles, forcing them to slow down – pulling out in front of an oncoming car when there are no other cars in sight and not increasing their speed; a more dangerous practice when merging on the expressway
- Drivers who don't yield when their lane is running out, preferring to pass all other cars waiting in line to try to get in front of them and risk an accident
- Drivers who block intersections or side streets while waiting for a light to change
- Drivers who cut off others in traffic, pulling into their lane without making sure there is enough room
- Driving too slow in the fast lane

• Tailgating – following too close behind a slower driver, although some people habitually drive that way; can be more dangerous when the driver in front further reduces speed or brakes suddenly, trying to get the tailgating car to back off

When anger takes over, our frustration is demonstrated by horn honking, tailgating, rude gestures, and perhaps running red lights and other traffic signs. Speeding is often involved, also changing lanes inappropriately to try to get in front of the slow driver.

These few minutes out of your life, stuck behind an inconsiderate driver, are not worth risking an accident. Relax and deal with it. Your anger is not going to change that person; it only makes you feel worse. *Police officers give tickets for aggressive driving.*

When the Driver is Already Angry

Everyone has either been an angry driver at some point or has ridden with one. Riding with an angry driver is scary. The passenger is scared of a crash and possibly scared of the driver. Teens, especially, need to stand up for themselves and refuse to ride with anyone who does not value the safety of his or her passengers.

Angry drivers need to realize the level of immaturity this reveals. While they might think it makes them look so worldly and experienced, they are actually telling everyone they just cannot cope with the demands of driving. Maturity is showing respect for your passengers' safety, for other drivers, and for your vehicle.

If angry when you get behind the wheel, your chance of having an accident improves dramatically. If you just had a fight with a loved one or had some tragic news, you are much more likely to drive faster or in a more reckless manner, but certainly less focused. Recklessness or lack of focus, while driving, greatly increases your possibility of getting a ticket and/or of having an accident.

Relax and Enjoy the Ride!

This is so important, and it is something we all know. If you drive like a crazy person, yelling at other drivers, speeding, pounding your hands on the steering wheel in frustration, how much better will that actually make you feel? How much faster will it get you where you want to go? That's right! We will not feel ANY better, nor will we reach our destination any quicker. In fact, we will feel worse as our anger intensifies, plus our chance of having an accident is much greater because we are driving aggressively.

Sometimes it helps to decide what is really important in your life. Is getting even with that driver who cut you off the most important thing? If you speed up to cut him off and possibly cause him to have a wreck, is that really going to make you feel like a great person? Although some things are intentional, sometimes a driver can simply make a mistake. Perhaps they did not check their blind spot and accidentally cut you off.

If you are driving slower than the person behind you wants to go, move over and let him pass. That might mean pulling into a side street or off the road. The question is: *Is it really worth having an accident?* Does it really matter to you if that person needs to go so fast? Perhaps they have an emergency. Give others the same consideration you would like to have.

If you are running late, plan better for the future and make sure you leave in plenty of time. Plan for possible delays if traveling during peak traffic times. Traffic will not move out of your way, so there is no need to get upset. Anger will not change anything except to possibly ruin your day, more so if you have an accident.

By giving others the benefit of the doubt and by choosing to be patient and courteous with others, you have a much greater chance of being an excellent, safe, respected driver.

Encounters with Angry Drivers

If you encounter an angry driver, put distance between you and that driver quickly. Do not make eye contact, flash your lights, make gestures, or do anything that could provoke a confrontation. You cannot know if that person is totally crazy. One small gesture might be enough to push him/her over the edge and reveal road rage smoldering inside. Do not take chances! If you feel threatened, call 911, but try to get away from that person as quickly as possible.

Driving is a privilege, not a right. Protect that privilege.
It provides a freedom not everyone can have.

Hello, Officer!

At some point, everyone will have an opportunity to talk to a police officer. Regardless of what has happened, how angry you might be (especially if you are speeding), who is at fault (accidents) and so on, it is in your best interest to be very polite to the officer.

When You Are Pulled Over

• Always greet the officer with respect: "Good morning/afternoon/evening, Officer." Always respond with "Sir" or "Ma'am" to any questions. Speak clearly and use proper English, no slang. Never refer to the officer as a "cop" and refrain from smart aleck comments about such things as quotas (that guarantees a ticket).

• The officer will ask for your license, car registration and proof of insurance. Tell him/her where it is located and ask for permission to get it. It is helpful to keep the registration and insurance info in an envelope in your glove box so you can find it easily.

• If you are stopped for speeding, you most likely were speeding. Radar guns are calibrated regularly and are probably more accurate than your car's speedometer. Asking when the gun was calibrated or other (irritating) questions will generally ensure getting a ticket.

• Once you realize an officer is pulling you over, signal to acknowledge him and look for a safe place to pull over. Pull well off the road to give him room to safely approach your car. Remain in your car, let the window down, and place both hands on top of the steering wheel as the officer approaches. This shows the officer you are not hiding anything.

• If stopped at night, turn on the interior/dome light.

• Laws vary from state to state but if you carry a weapon, it may be necessary to disclose that information. Know the carry laws in your state.

Regardless of why you were stopped: speeding, running a red light, making an illegal turn, etc., take responsibility for making a bad decision and be polite. The officer might allow you to give a reason for your action. While you may get a ticket, by showing respect and accepting responsibility, you might just get a warning. Either way, you should feel better about handling the issue in a mature manner.

Whether or not you get a ticket, it is best to accept the situation as a minor setback, a bad decision on your part, and not let it ruin your day. Remember, the same officer who gave you a speeding ticket could also be the one who responded to a dangerous home invasion call and put his life on the line the night before.

In other words, nobody is out to get you; the officer is doing the job he or she was hired to do. They are people, just like everyone else – not policing robots without feelings. Like the rest of us, they have personal lives, families, problems, and good and bad days.

Unlike the rest of us, they have taken an oath to "Protect and Serve." The police/911 is the first call we make if we are in trouble. Tickets are inconvenient, but we certainly want their help if something bad happens. No, every single one of them is not perfect (just as no one else is perfect) but they deserve our respect.

How to Avoid Getting a Ticket

• "Move Over Law" – Are you familiar with the *Move Over Law*? Move over for emergency responders, or you may get a ticket. This law has now been adopted in every state except for Washington, D.C. This law requires drivers to move over into the other lane (if possible) or to significantly slow their speed any time a police officer or other emergency responder, including tow trucks or other recovery vehicles, are on the side of the road.

Laws vary from state to state. For example, some states require drivers to reduce their speed 10 mph, some 20 mph. Also, be prepared to stop. Google *Move Over Law* for your state or check this AAA website: http://drivinglaws.aaa.com/laws/move-over-law/

• On multi-lane roads, don't drive in the "fast" lane (inside far left). Driving in the fast lane means you might be speeding and causes them to check. Some states have passed a law where slow drivers will be ticketed for impeding traffic flow by driving in the fast lane.

- Never be the fastest driver and don't drive more than ten miles over the speed limit. Some police departments do not ticket for 10 and under (over the speed limit), but City Police and State Troopers can generally ticket for any speed over the posted speed limit.

- Throwing a cigarette butt out of your car window could result in a ticket for littering (could be a substantial fine).

- Police will stop cars that have any non-working lights, including a burned out car tag light.

- Tickets for speeding in a school zone are VERY expensive.

- Tickets given for running stop signs in neighborhoods are also expensive. Basically, avoid tickets by always obeying traffic signs or signals of any type.

- Flashing your headlights to warn oncoming drivers of a police car up ahead can result in a ticket. Also, what if the police were watching for a stolen car or kidnapper – and your flashing headlights warned the criminals, allowing them to get away?

- It is illegal to pass on the right in most states except when there is sufficient pavement width for both your car and the one making the left turn. It is illegal to travel on the shoulder of the road.

- It is amazing how many people still text while driving. While everyone admits it is dangerous, many seem to think they could never have or cause an accident. If the conversation is that important, pull off to the side of the road and finish it safely.

- Wear your seat belt. Most states have seat belt laws for front and back seats, and those laws are enforced. While most people automatically buckle up any time they get into a car, this safety feature is apparently still disregarded by some. Roadside signs saying "Buckle Up" and "Click It or Ticket" tell us there are still people who refuse to wear seat belts.

Real case: An 18 year old girl lost control of her car and crashed. Not wearing her seatbelt, she regained consciousness only to find her head stuck in her windshield. The car could not be seen from the road. She was incredibly fortunate, not only to have minor injuries but to be able to reach her cell phone and call for help. However, if she had been wearing her seatbelt, her face would not have been imbedded in the windshield.

New source of tickets: unsafe driving around big trucks
Special Rules for Semi-Trucks/Tractor Trailers
In some states, tickets are issued for driving in an unsafe manner around big trucks. A fully loaded tractor trailer traveling at 55mph needs three times the distance a car needs to stop. These trucks also have large blind spots on both sides as well as at the rear of the truck. Basically, if you cannot see the driver's face in his side mirror, he cannot see you.

Many accidents occur each year because of drivers ignoring the travel needs of the big trucks. Pulling out in front of a tractor trailer and then slamming on your brakes can cause the truck to jackknife. This action can have disastrous effects, causing huge accidents that often kill the driver of the car who cut the truck off. Because of these types of accidents, police watch for drivers who ignore truck safety.

Big Truck Safety
Leave plenty of room when pulling in front of semi-trucks and use your blinkers. For safety, one car length of space for every 10mph of speed is recommended.

Do not tailgate. Big trucks cannot see cars driving too close behind them; it is a blind spot. Also, if you are tailgating, you cannot see what is happening with the traffic ahead. If the truck brakes suddenly, you have no time to react and no place to go.

When to Call 511

A relative newcomer to the traffic scene, 511 is gaining more recognition as they continue to add important services. 511 is not offered in every state at this time, but service is state- or city-specific, meaning you receive information for the state or city you are in when you dial 511. Basic information is available from the U.S. Department of Transportation Federal Highway Administration website: *http://www.fhwa.dot.gov/trafficinfo/511.htm.*

In Georgia, for example, you can dial 511 from a cell phone or land line to access information. To find your state's 511 website (if operational), type the state name and 511 in your browser (Georgia 511). Standard cell phone rates apply when calling 511. Check out the Georgia 511 website: *http://www.511ga.org.* You will be impressed with the information and many services available.

Services include current traffic and accident information. For example, if traffic is not moving on the expressway at 10 p.m., call 511 to learn if there is a major accident, construction, etc. Get information on road closures, weather, road conditions, road construction updates, and detailed weather reports.

An important service offered by Georgia 511 (and some other states) are the Hero Units. HEROs (Highway Emergency Response Operators) provide assistance to motorists with vehicle problems. Overall 511 goals include diminishing disruption of expressway traffic and relieving congestion due to vehicle problems. *Known as HEROs in Georgia, called by other names in different states.*

The HERO Units patrol Atlanta-area expressways weekdays from 5:30 a.m. to 9 p.m. and weekends from 7:30 a.m. to 9 p.m. and are on call for incidents occurring outside of regular operating hours. Additionally, they provide assistance to law enforcement and emergency personnel and assist in clearing stalled vehicles from travel lanes. They help stranded motorists with minor mechanical problems including changing flat tires, jump starting weak batteries, providing fuel/coolant/other fluids, transportation to safer areas, and courtesy use of a telephone. *Note: HEROs do not provide wrecker services. (source: http://www.511ga.org).*

Are You a Great Driver?

Most of us believe we are great drivers; however, everyone complains about how people drive. Does it seem more and more drivers are unaware of driving rules? And of common courtesy?

The following points do not include every single known safety tip, only those that seem to be disregarded most often. So, are you really a great driver? How do you rate on these points?

• Emergency vehicles always have the right of way. When you hear a siren or see a police car responding to a silent alarm, STOP – preferably off the road to give the police/fire truck/ambulance a clear lane. Your radio should never be too loud to hear a siren.

• Always wear your seat belt. Most accidents happen within a few miles of your home.

• Never leave your car running/unlocked while you run into a store for "just a second," especially with a child in the car.

• Pedestrians and bicycle riders always have the right of way. *Note to pedestrians and bicycle riders: walk or ride where you are supposed to be. Vehicles may not be able to see you, especially at night. Use crosswalks and watch out for your own safety. Wear clothing that makes you easy to see (do not wear dark clothes at night), and bicycles should have reflectors and lights for night riding.*

• Do not use Cruise Control when it is raining; your vehicle is more likely to hydroplane. Also, do not use Cruise Control if roads have ice or snow on them.

• If using your lights on high beam, be sure to switch to low beams when cars approach or when you are behind another car.

• When driving in fog, always keep your lights on low beam.

• Children are safer riding in the back seat in seat belts or car seats. If your vehicle has air bags, manufacturers warn that children aged 12 and under can be *killed* when the front seat air bag deploys at 80 mph. Some foreign countries have the right idea: children ages 12 and younger are not allowed to travel in the front seat.

• Always use your blinker so other drivers know your plans. That is your responsibility as a driver. Blinkers should be on at least 50 feet from where you plan to turn – not after you apply your brakes and begin to turn. If you are hit from behind and have not properly used your blinker, it can be your fault.

• When planning to turn right, but not at the next street, watch the cars at streets before your turn. A driver trying to enter traffic from a side street does not know if you intend to turn there or somewhere further down the road.

If you are waiting: When at a side street and an oncoming car has its blinker on, do not assume it will turn at your street. That driver could be planning to turn at the next street past yours. Wait until the driver begins to turn before pulling out in front of that car.

• On four lane roads, slower drivers should stay to the right; the left lane is for passing. If someone is in a hurry, be respectful and courteous – move to the other lane (or pull off to the side on two lane roads) and let them pass.

This is especially true for cell phone drivers who get in the left (fast) lane and drive well below the speed limit as they carry on in-depth conversations.

• If traffic lights are available, use them when making a left turn out of a store or gas station in a busy area. Many accidents happen when drivers try to cross multiple lanes of traffic. Do not take the chance of endangering yourself or others.

• Cell Phones: Studies show that drivers on cell phones have the same response time as a drunk driver. If you must use your cell phone while driving, stay in the right lane so you do not impede the flow of traffic – or even better, pull off the road to finish your call.

If you are in an accident, insurance companies can access your cell phone records. If you were talking on the phone or texting when or immediately before the accident occurred, the insurance company could refuse to pay your claim.

• YIELD means let the other traffic go ahead of you. A YIELD sign leading onto a four lane road (two lanes on each side) means you *wait* until the oncoming traffic is finished – even though there are two lanes on your side. If there is a sign that says "Keep Moving," you do not have to stop. Even when there is no YIELD sign (like when leaving your driveway), you must yield to the oncoming traffic.

• When you know the lane ahead is going to end, YIELD to the drivers in the other lane. Put on your blinker and wait for a safe opportunity to move into the other lane. Plan ahead to avoid causing a traffic bottleneck when the lane ends – and risking an accident by trying to force your way in.

• All vehicles have blind spots. Locate them on your car and adjust your mirrors. Also, pay attention to cars around you when changing lanes, and look over your shoulder as needed.

• Watch traffic carefully before pulling out in front of an oncoming car. Is anyone behind them? If only one car is coming, wait until it passes. Do not pull out and cause them to slow down. If you do pull out in front of them, increase your speed quickly.

Too often, drivers pull out in front of an oncoming car when they should have waited. This is more important when a large truck or tractor trailer is coming. The weight of the truck requires a longer time to stop, and you could cause a major accident (possibly fatal) by thinking a truck can stop as quickly as a small car.

Bad weather and rain or snow slick roads require a longer stopping time for all vehicles, but especially for heavy trucks.

• Watch cars entering traffic from side streets; they might pull out in front of you and require you to slow down quickly or stop.

- When driving behind a large truck, van or SUV, we frequently cannot see the brake lights or blinkers of a car in front of that larger vehicle. Stay back so there is plenty of room to stop.

  If you are driving the larger vehicle, let the drivers behind you know the car ahead is getting ready to turn or stop. Steer your vehicle slightly to the left or right so the drivers behind you can see the front car's blinker or brake lights – or turn on your blinker so the cars behind know they need to slow down.

- Another way to alert drivers behind you is to pump your brakes several times. They will not know why you are doing that, but the flashing brake lights will tell them to slow down. Many rear end collisions could be avoided if drivers of large vehicles would let the cars behind them know what is happening up ahead.

- 5 Second Rule: Check to see if you are following too close to the car in front of you. How long will it take you to stop? Pick a non-moving object (sign or pole). Count seconds (1001, 1002...) when the car ahead of you passes the object. Stop counting when your car passes the same object.

  The number of seconds counted is how long it will take to stop your car if the car in front stops suddenly. This should be a minimum of five seconds (translates to five car lengths) to keep from hitting the car in front of you.

- Share the road! Part of responsible driving is awareness of merging traffic. If someone needs to enter traffic on a highway, change lanes if you can do so safely and let them in. To change lanes, be a courteous driver and pass the cars trying to enter traffic (from side streets or expressway ramps) before moving into their lane.

- When there is an obstacle in your lane (mail truck, stopped car, bag of trash, etc.), yield to oncoming traffic as you plan to go around the obstacle. By law, you can pass the obstruction only when your view is clear, then you should drive at a reduced speed. Also, only the car immediately behind the obstacle may pass. Do not pull out to pass a line of cars.

- When coming to a stop in traffic, stop far enough back to see the full rear wheels of the vehicle in front of you. That way, if the car behind happens to bump you, it won't push you into the car in front – and the police officer called to the accident will not give you a ticket for following too close. Also, if the car ahead of you breaks down or if there is any danger, you will have room to pull around it.

- When stopping at an intersection, if the car in front of you is too far out into the intersection, leave room in case they cannot turn and need to back up. Also, if a car hits them, you will not also be involved in the accident (following too close).

- Most red lights are 30 seconds to two minutes in length – not nearly as long as it seems when you are waiting. While it may be inconvenient to stop and start again, nothing is worth risking an accident. At a stop sign or right-turn-on-red, stop and count three seconds (1001, 1002, 1003) before going.

- At a four-way stop, the first car to come to a FULL stop is the one who goes first. If two cars arrive at a stop sign at the same time, yield to the car on your right.

- When in a line of traffic, never block intersections, and try not to block entrances into businesses and side streets.

- School Bus Laws – All states require traffic following school buses to stop when the bus STOP sign is out to the side. Most states require oncoming traffic to also stop, even on four lane roads, unless there is a concrete median. When in doubt, stop. School bus and school zone tickets are always expensive.

- Yield to all highway maintenance workers and vehicles in a construction zone. Road crews should be given the same respect as a police officer directing traffic. In most states, that is law; you can be reported and ticketed for failure to acknowledge the crewman directing traffic. Even if it is not a law in your state, do it anyway. Many road crew workers are killed each year by careless drivers.

- Try not to drive behind trucks loaded with items. Whether work tools or household goods (including mattresses), sometimes the items are not well secured. Particularly with expressway driving, an item could fly off and hit your car, or cause a wreck and kill you. Ladders are especially dangerous. Whenever you are hauling anything, always make sure it is tied down very well.

- When someone lets you cut in front of them, take a moment to wave back and thank them.

- Laws change over the years. Everyone should review the State Driver's Manual periodically to avoid unexpected tickets. Not knowing the law will not keep you from getting a ticket.

The Truth about Headlights

Most drivers think the primary purpose of headlights is to see where they are going. Lights are more helpful on dark roads but in well-lit areas, some people forget to make sure their headlights are even on! Headlights are a safety feature so *other drivers can see you*. If you do not use your headlights at all times, at least do this:

When it is raining, turn your lights on.

At dusk or dawn, turn your lights on.

On cloudy or foggy days, turn your lights on.

Gray, tan and dark colored vehicles without lights are even more difficult to see at dusk, sunrise, or in bad weather. If you have an accident with a car that did not have headlights on, be sure to take a picture with your cell phone and to tell the police.

Lights on during the day: Several studies have shown that during daylight driving, the subconscious mind is more aware of cars with headlights on. Also, when drivers travel into direct sun, they are less able to see oncoming vehicles. However, if oncoming cars have their lights on, they are easily seen. To lessen your chance of an accident, drive with your headlights on at all times.

Good to Know

- If you are running low on gas, turn off your air conditioner (A/C) and slow your speed. The A/C can make your engine work harder and use more gas.

  Studies show that on short trips, running your A/C uses more gas. However, for expressway driving, the A/C actually uses less gas than having windows down because of wind resistance.

  If your car is overheating, turn off your A/C.

- When starting your car, turn to ON and wait 15 seconds before starting (or until the chiming stops). All cars can benefit from this procedure, but computer chips in cars today need a few moments to engage and identify the systems before starting the engine.

- After starting your car, let it idle a minute before putting it in gear. Fluids need time to circulate through the engine before turning on the heat, A/C, or defroster. This is especially important for the A/C and transmission fluids. In winter, driving too fast when the engine is cold may cause a blown head gasket.

- To extend the life of your transmission, come to a complete stop before changing gears. Always use the emergency brake when parking the car. Even a slight slope puts pressure on the transmission, and it will last longer if the emergency brake is used. It is best to not routinely park on a slope; try to park in a flat area.

- Avoid "Jack Rabbit" starts. Hard acceleration causes the car to lurch forward – bad for the transmission and gas mileage.

- Use less gas by reducing speed. Accelerate slowly from a stop and slow down gradually when coming to a red light or stop sign. "Coast" by not accelerating (do not put car in N - neutral) to save money on gas. Rather than speeding up to the light, then braking, slow down when coming to a red light or stop sign. It saves on gas *and* on repairs by not wearing out brakes as quickly.

- Improve gas mileage and prevent other costly problems by using the tachometer (usually to the left of the speedometer). When accelerating from a stop, the tach should show between 2 – 3 RPMs (actually 2000-3000). When possible, keeping the tach needle below 2000 RPMs is even better for saving gas. It might be helpful to move your heel off the gas pedal (a few inches out in front of it) if you tend to be a heavy-footed driver.

- Always make sure the gas cap is tight when you get fuel. A loose cap can cause the Check Engine Light to come on, as well as allow gasoline to evaporate from your tank.

- When parking in hot sun, use a sun deflector to protect the dash from cracking and bleaching as well as to help cool the car. If in a safe area, lower your windows ¼ to ½ inch to allow hot air to escape.

- Windshield wipers should be replaced when they smear the windshield. Do not buy the cheapest wipers; they don't last long. Buy a good name, medium-priced brand. Keep your receipt to make sure the wipers last as long as the manufacturer says they will. Get a hand-written receipt (or photocopy your receipt) because information disappears from the machine-printed thermal paper receipts.

- Use the forms in the back of this book to record all services and purchases for your car. Keep the book in your glove box so it is always handy. Keeping a service record is also a good sales tool.

- In dry weather, wipers last longer if the rubber part (blade) is treated with ArmorAll or a similar product. The wipes are very handy or use the spray bottle and a soft cloth.

- Vehicle Emissions – when taking your vehicle to be inspected, drive at 40 - 50mph for 15 minutes or more before having it inspected so the car can burn off impurities that collect while not being driven. This is particularly important if the vehicle is older and there is concern as to whether it will pass the emissions inspection.

- Always keep your gasoline level above 1/4 tank, a half tank is even better. Running out of gas could leave you stranded in a bad or desolate area or perhaps force you to buy gas at a place where you would rather not stop. Be prepared for situations when you might not have time to get gas or could get caught in a bad traffic jam.

Experts recommend gas tanks be kept full. Condensation occurs in a partially-filled tank; that water can rust the tank over time. Gas cools the fuel pump. Driving on a regular basis at 1/4 tank or below can cause the fuel pump to become clogged or burned out.

Many of us cannot afford to keep our tanks filled, but we should try to fill up at least occasionally. Another idea is to fill your tank and re-fill when it reaches the halfway mark instead of waiting until it is empty.

- If you have car trouble and leave the hazard lights (4-way flashers) on, the lights will continue to use power from the battery. If you are gone for any length of time, you may need jumper cables and assistance (or a jump box) to start a dead battery.

- Many vehicles have magnetic decals. We proudly show various causes we support along with soccer balls, baseballs, and more. When cars are in the sun, they are continually being bleached. If the decals are never moved, one day you will move them to find darker paint under the decal. If there is a chance you might someday want to sell or trade in the car – or if you have a leased car, you should remove the decals or change their location frequently.

It is best to remove magnetic decals before having wax applied so they are not sealed to your car.

- Either at the drive-through car wash or by hand, have wax applied to your car at least twice a year to protect the paint. If spray wax (from a car wash) is applied too often, a film can build up on your windshield. Remove it by cleaning with a Windex-type product.

- If you don't have a specialty/status tag, do you know your tag number? Take a close-up photo with your cell phone and keep it saved. Parents should keep a photo of all family car tags in their phone. Whether completing a form that requires the information or, worst case, a car is stolen, having that car tag number at your fingertips could be invaluable.

• Keep the number of a towing service in your car, also a list of important phone numbers – just in case that need ever arises and your cell phone isn't an option.

• When giving someone directions, always include landmarks and an idea of the mileage, possible traffic conditions or known roadwork, and length of time it might take. Even if they are using a GPS, some areas are not mapped correctly.

• If your car is parked in a heavily wooded area, be aware that mice/rats and other critters could choose to live in the engine area – and they can do a LOT of damage.

Imagine the scene in an upscale Mercedes service shop one day when a lady came in because her Check Engine Light was on. She was watching from the viewing room as technicians suddenly began running everywhere, chasing the rats that had exited her car. The wiring damage cost thousands of dollars, thankfully covered by her car insurance.

Foggy Headlights

If your vehicle is older and a film has developed on the plastic headlight cover, there are several products that can make the lights look almost brand new! The *3M Headlight Restoration Kit* is excellent. Once the painted area is taped off, it takes less than 30 minutes for great results. Available at auto supply stores.

Ignition Problems

If your key won't turn, there are several things to check.
• Usually, the steering wheel has locked in a "safety" mode. Use pressure to "jiggle" the wheel back and forth until the key will work.
• With an automatic transmission, the key will not turn if the car was not left in "P" (Park) when it was turned off.
• Check your key to make sure it is flat and not bent.

- If none of the above suggestions work, and if you have not lubricated your ignition (applying oil in the slot where the key goes), a spray of oil could save the day. Graphite lubricant is preferable, but WD-40 will work. Be sure to lubricate all hinges and locks at least twice a year. This includes hood, trunk or tailgate, all door hinges, door locks, and gas cap door.

Remote Openers

- If you forget where you are parked, press the "lock" button on your remote. The horn beeps and flashing lights will lead you to your car.
- If your remote still works but the car no longer beeps when the lock button is pressed, the remote can often be reset by pressing the lock and unlock buttons at the same time. Hold for a few seconds. If that doesn't work, ask your dealership to reset it for you.
- If the remote opener is slow to respond or stops working, it may need a new battery. Auto supply stores stock these batteries and are usually happy to replace it for you. Batteries can also be purchased at your dealership.
- If the remote totally stops working (light doesn't flash even with a new battery), replacements can be purchased through a dealer. However, also look online, especially on eBay, to see if there are used remotes for your car. You might save more than $100. Depending on the instructions, you might need to take the new/used remote to the dealer to have it reset.

Aftermarket remotes might work, but make sure there is a good return policy before buying an aftermarket product.

Keep a Record of Problems

If your vehicle starts making unusual sounds or having other problems, keep a record of when it started and how things progress. Use the "Notes" pages in the back of this book or keep a separate small notebook in your car. Just as your doctor will ask, "How long has this been going on?", your mechanic will want that same information about problems with your car.

What You Need to Know About Repairs

Dealerships, Mechanics & Other Shops

Your car/truck/SUV/van needs service. Where do you go? It is best to get a referral from a friend, neighbor or co-worker, or you can look for feedback online. Over the years, the auto repair industry developed a reputation for taking advantage of people. According to numerous sources, men, even if they are not car-savvy, are less likely to be taken advantage of than women and the elderly. But like many other industries, there are good and bad folks and you must find people you trust.

Become an informed shopper by asking questions. For major repairs, get at least two written estimates. Be sure your estimates are comparable – either both use factory parts or both use aftermarket parts. If you are not working with a dealership, be sure your final bill lists every part and service performed. Know if there is a warranty for the work, how long the warranty is for, and keep your receipt.

Note: "aftermarket" parts are made to replace factory parts, generally at a much reduced price (but not always). Sometimes, aftermarket parts are just fine. Other times, they might not perform as long as the factory part, or they might not perform as well.

Before You Need a Major Repair

It is best to establish a repair relationship before you need a major repair. Select a shop and have minor things done (oil change, tires rotated, etc.) to "test the water." Is the work performed in a timely manner? Is your car left clean? Do they always try to sell you something else? If they always try to "up sell" (sell you something you may not need), you might want to find a new shop.

When dealing with car repairs, again, the most important issue is finding someone you trust. (*Trust* will come up often in this section.) Then, if your trusted mechanic or dealership service advisor tells you it is time to change fluids, belts, etc., you know they are telling you the truth.

Also, it is good to note that loyalty is generally rewarded. Whether you are a regular customer at a dealership, an independent mechanic or another shop, your loyalty to them will result in better service and discounts.

When You Need a Major Repair
When you need a major repair, always ask questions:
- What happened?
- What caused it to happen?
- Why do I need this?
- How can I prevent this from happening again?
- Is there a warranty?
- Does this make sense? *(ask yourself this question)*

and...How much will it cost?

How Much Will It Cost?
Be wary of advertised prices that are "too good to be true." You will likely sign something with fine print stating that other charges may apply once they actually get the part out of your car and find other damage – damage they know will be there. Once your transmission is lying in pieces on the floor, you are stuck. Instead, be sure you are dealing with a reputable place from the beginning.

Dealerships have a suggested retail price and a marked up price (matrix) for customers. All dealerships do not charge the same matrix price. Independent mechanics write their quotes using the dealership's matrix price as a guide. An independent mechanic does not have the overhead costs a dealership has, so he may have more room to negotiate pricing. The dealership, however, may be more concerned with and more knowledgeable about keeping your car in pristine factory condition.

When comparing quotes, ask if the independent mechanic is using factory parts (bought from a dealership) or if he is using aftermarket parts. Sometimes dealership prices are less expensive than aftermarket parts, and some mechanics will allow customers to purchase the parts and only charge for the labor to install the parts.

Ask questions. Be sure your quotes compare "apples to apples." It could be a better immediate financial decision to go with the best price; however, be sure the aftermarket parts will not affect the operations of your particular vehicle.

While not always practical, keep your old parts if you have any suspicions about the repair or the possible quality of the repair. If something comes up later and you end up at another repair shop, that mechanic might be able to see what happened.

Bottom line: when taking your car in for a major repair, listen to what they say and decide if it makes sense. Ask questions, know prices, and make an informed decision.

DEALERSHIPS – *What you need to know*

Dealerships are generally able to stand behind their work in cases where independent mechanics and other shops may not. Also, because dealership mechanics are familiar with a particular make of car, they may be aware of failures not covered in the Owner's Manual and not known by those outside the dealership.

For example, while the manual may recommend a service at a specific mileage point, dealership mechanics have the advantage of experience. They might know that replacing certain fluids *prior* to the recommended time may save the customer a lot of money on replacement parts.

Dealerships employ a range of expertise from your basic new trainee (changes oil, replaces headlights, etc.) to master mechanics who are paid for their extensive knowledge. Because dealerships provide a nice facility with a comfy lounge and restrooms, certified mechanics, service advisors, office staff, porters, etc., the dealership may be more expensive.

Dealerships use only factory parts, and their labor cost may be higher. That said, studies have shown cars generally last longer when consistently supplied with factory parts and service. For example, when an auto maker develops a new oil filter system (or other parts), that design is patented. While aftermarket products might be very similar to the patented design, they cannot be exactly the same. By using factory parts, your car will stay in optimal running condition.

Much of the time, particularly for older cars, aftermarket parts are fine. We will not discuss individual car makers, but a trusted service advisor at your dealership or a reputable independent mechanic can offer good information.

Dealership service advisors work on commission. When your car is serviced, the mechanic will list anything the car might need. Service advisors are paid a percentage of the repair cost. While most are very honest, there are unscrupulous people in every line of work. If your car seems to need multiple repairs every time you visit the service department, or if it seems you are getting strong-armed into expensive repair decisions, you might want to think about getting a second opinion.

Although dealerships keep a computer record of all service performed, you should also keep a record of all services and purchases for your car. Use the handy forms in the back of this book. Then if someone says, "You need new brakes, air filter, wipers, etc.," you can check the book and know exactly when you last had that item serviced or replaced. Keeping a list of services and purchases is also a great selling tool when you decide to sell or trade in your car.

MECHANICS – *What you need to know*

When choosing a mechanic, it is especially important to have a referral because there are no regulations for this industry. Anyone can hang a sign advertising car repair. Independent mechanics can be a one or two person operation or a large shop. Many people like the personal service offered by a smaller business.

Mechanics often specialize in either domestic (U.S. made) or foreign cars, although there are shops that do both. Foreign cars generally require a different set of tools (metric) and knowledge. Before taking your car in for service, know if that mechanic can actually work on your car.

If you have a new car, you will take it to the dealership for service. With older cars, you may find that a good mechanic will charge less for the same work. Mechanics can also perform warranty work that will not void your warranty. Just be sure you keep all the paperwork. Warranty work done by an independent mechanic (or even a friend) should be valid as long as it is dated, car mileage noted, etc. *Check with your dealership for warranty specifics.*

Again, as with any type of service, trust is the key to a successful transaction. You might not know the shop is saving money by using aftermarket parts (and perhaps charging for factory parts). Is this discouraging? Yes. Unfortunately, unless you are able to repair your own car, you are at the mercy of those who provide that service – which is why it is so important to give your business to someone you trust.

Be sure your final bill lists the parts used, particularly if you are charged for factory parts. That could be important later if something breaks and another mechanic tells you factory parts were not actually used.

Do as much research as you can, and always deal with people you trust.

OTHER SHOPS – *What you need to know*

There are many shops that advertise repairs for brakes, oil changes, transmissions, tire sales, body work, etc. and do other repairs along with the work advertised in their name. Some of these shops seem to have a more aggressive approach to up selling; however, qualified mechanics and good workmanship can be found at any shop. Again, the most important part of car repair is to find someone you trust. Referrals are always a good starting point.

FRIENDS – *What you need to know*

Friends who work on cars can save us a lot of money – as long as they know exactly what they are doing. However, if anything does not work right or causes more problems, you may lose that friendship – or worse. Also, it is good to check prices even when friends do you a "favor." Sometimes it may not be as good a deal as you think.

Warning: never let your car be your friend's first brake job!

Regardless where the work is done, regular maintenance will make the vehicle last longer and can help you avoid unnecessary repairs.

Basic Maintenance Checklist

The following information is meant as a guide and does not replace the Owner's Manual. Refer to the Owner's Manual for information specific to your car. Manuals can be ordered from dealerships or online sources.

The *Basic Maintenance Checklist* (see forms in back of book) lists things that should be checked regularly. If you don't know where everything is located, have someone show you. Your mechanic is a great source, or search online with Google and YouTube videos. On YouTube, type in what you want, like: *how to check transmission fluid.* Answers should also be in the Owner's Manual; however, it might be easier to understand if you see someone do it on YouTube or if someone shows you.

Another option is an auto parts store. Buy a quart of oil (ask what kind to buy), then ask them to show you how to check and add oil. Even if you don't need oil, he will show you how to add it. While the hood is open, ask how to check the other fluids, including windshield washing fluid. If you need new wiper blades, those stores usually offer free installation.

Save money and make your car last longer by keeping fluid levels full and changed as needed. When you have the oil changed, ask them to check the fluid levels. Some shops charge extra to top off fluids. Ignoring these seemingly small items, especially oil and filter changes, can create expensive problems like causing your engine to "seize up" (basically, that means the engine melts).

Using the Checklist

For older cars, go through this Checklist at least once each month. If your car tends to use oil, run hot or have other problems, it may be good to check everything twice a month (perhaps on the first and fifteenth days of the month). If the car has an ongoing problem, weekly or daily checks might be needed. If that is the case, it is really important to get the car serviced before it quits. For newer cars, every three months (or when you get your oil changed) should be fine.

Always fully check out your car before going on a long trip.

Fluids

Check fluid levels when the engine is cold (not driven for several hours). The car must be parked on level ground. If any fluids are low, keep a close watch on that particular fluid to determine if it is leaking and if your car needs service.

Fluid Leaks: Not sure if your car has a leak? Open a cardboard box flat and slide the inside (without writing) under your engine area. It will be easy to see any problem with leaks.

Take the box to your mechanic. He might be able to identify the problem by seeing where the fluid is on the box if you can show him where the box was placed. Be sure to designate right/left and how far back the box was placed from the front bumper of the car.

Antifreeze/Coolant. In summer, this important fluid keeps your car from overheating. In winter, it keeps your radiator from freezing (and cracking = new radiator). The shop that changes your oil should make sure your antifreeze is the right mix.

Check antifreeze level when engine is cold – never while the engine is hot. If hot, let the engine cool for at least thirty minutes before opening the cap. Be sure you are checking the radiator (usually the front center of the motor area) and not the overflow tank.

Unscrew radiator cap and look inside. The fluid level should be just below the neck of the tank (where the cap screws on). If the fluid level is down, add a 50/50 mixture of coolant and water (or use the premixed kind). Depending on your vehicle, coolant should be bright green or orange-red, and it should look rather clear, not cloudy. If coolant looks dirty or cloudy, or if there is rust or other debris floating in it, this could indicate a problem elsewhere in the engine and should be checked immediately.

Loss of coolant should be investigated. It could be something big (head gasket problem) or something minor (pinhole leak or loose hose connection). Catching small problems early can help prevent expensive repairs later.

NOTE: Never remove the radiator cap when the engine is hot or overheating. If the gauge in your car shows hot, pull off to the side of the road and stop the vehicle. If the radiator is making whistling or sizzling noises (like a tea kettle), do not open the hood until the engine has cooled.

Never fill your radiator with water unless it is an emergency. The tank may have to be drained to add the appropriate fluid/water mix.

Antifreeze is poisonous to humans and pets.

Brake Fluid. Look for the "add" line. If fluid is lower than the "add" line, add the appropriate fluid for your vehicle. Brake fluid can decrease slightly as brakes wear. If it is low, your mechanic must determine if there is a leak or if the brakes are wearing. Brake fluid should be changed about every two years or as recommended by your mechanic or service advisor.

Oil. If a car runs out of oil, it will destroy the engine. Especially with an older car, check the oil regularly. The oil and filter should be changed every 3,000 miles, although some say 4-5,000 miles for lighter driving. Regular oil changes at 3,000 miles are good insurance for a healthy engine. *If you go a few hundred miles over 3000, it is not a big problem.*

An old mechanic once said, "Oil is the life blood of your engine. Clean oil is like having a healthy heart." Get your oil and filter changed regularly at a reputable place, not the cheapest.

Dealerships and independent mechanics do more than just change oil; they check other fluid levels and do a general inspection of the car. It is best to always have your oil changed at the same place.

How to check and add oil: the oil stick/dipstick is usually the most prominent "stick." Remove stick, wipe with paper towel or rag, and then re-insert the stick.

There are two circles or two lines on the stick. The bottom circle or line (closest to the wet end of the stick) is the "add" line. The top circle or line is the "full" line. If the oil shows at the "add" mark, you need to add *some* oil but not the entire bottle. Pour about half the bottle in, wait five minutes, then do the stick test again. DO NOT overfill the oil.

To add oil, open hood and look for a large rectangular "box" (sometimes more square in smaller cars) usually located in the center of the engine area. On that "box," there will be a round cap with writing on it. It might say, "Add Oil" on the cap. Twist off the cap and pour oil into the hole.

MAKE SURE you are pouring oil into the right place. If you have any doubt, ask someone or watch a YouTube video on adding oil.

A funnel helps pour oil without spilling. If oil spills, the engine may smoke while oil residue burns off; however, it does not cause damage. Spills can be wiped off with a paper towel or rag.

After an oil change, check your oil. Occasionally, shops make mistakes. If there is a burning smell, check to see if oil was spilled or the cap or stick was left out. If other parts appear wet, have your oil filter checked. Filters can go bad and leak. If this isn't caught quickly, other parts of the engine could be damaged.

Power Steering Fluid. This fluid is usually in a container or reservoir with add/full markings on the side, or there may be a dipstick inside the container. Add fluid if necessary. Power Steering Fluid should be changed about every two years or as recommended by your mechanic or service advisor.

NOTE: If car is hard to steer, check this fluid immediately. If the fluid level is low, check it often to make sure it is not leaking.

Transmission Fluid. Maintaining this fluid is important to make your transmission last. Check your Owner's Manual (or Google for info) to know where this container/reservoir is located. Some vehicles have a dipstick; others do not. The engine should be idling when this fluid is checked.

Know when this fluid should be changed for your specific vehicle, or ask your mechanic or service advisor.

New transmission fluid has no smell and is a clear red color. Old fluid might have a mild burnt smell. Brown or black fluid can indicate trouble with your transmission. This is an important item to note when buying a used car.

Hardware

Air Conditioner. Even in cold weather, run the air conditioner once a month for at least a minute to circulate oil through the system. If left sitting too long, oil can settle in the compressor and cause the air conditioner to quit working. A dirty cabin air filter can also affect performance.

Air Filters. There are two types of air filters: one is the internal combustion air filter that keeps particles from getting into the engine, and the other is an air conditioning or cabin filter. Every car does not have a cabin filter; check the Owner's Manual or Google that question if you do not know about your particular vehicle. Both filters are important and should be replaced when the Owner's Manual advises.

The air combustion filter is a favorite "up sell" at repair shops. Know when your vehicle's filter is supposed to be changed. It is also easy and cheap to buy the filter from an auto parts store and change that filter yourself (check YouTube videos).

Alignment. When cars are out of alignment, tires wear out more quickly. If tires are wearing unevenly, your car may need alignment. If your car runs rough on some roads, your tires might need to be rotated or balanced.

To check your alignment, drive at 40mph on a straight road. With no cars behind you, use brake pedal and reduce your speed quickly to about 15 mph. If the car pulls to the right or left, it could need an alignment. Your mechanic can properly advise you.

Battery. If your car is slow to start, the battery may be going bad. Have it checked *before* you get stranded. Auto parts stores usually have a battery testing machine, as do mechanics and dealerships. See chapter on batteries for more information about care and use.

Belts. A favorite quick-profit item at repair shops, do not replace belts unless your *trusted* mechanic or service advisor says it is necessary.

Brakes. Your mechanic should keep an eye on your brakes as you have routine service done (like oil changes). If your brakes are making any type of noise, have them checked immediately. If the brake pedal is getting low, feeling "mushy" or you must pump your brake pedal to stop, the front brakes probably need service. Replacing brake pads is not a major expense, generally around $100 or so ($100 for front, and $100 for rear). If you wait until there is a metal or grinding sound, the rotors may be damaged and the price will soar into hundreds of dollars.

Check Engine Light. If the *Check Engine* light comes on, have that checked very quickly. The light could mean something insignificant, like a past due oil change or a loose gas cap, or it could mean there is a major problem. *When that light comes on, always check your oil level.* Do not take a chance of having a major repair on your car. Have that alert checked out as soon as possible by your mechanic or dealership.

Engine Noise. If the engine starts making a strange noise, have it checked out. Our cars often warn us with noises before quitting. Do not ignore noises coming from your engine or brakes.

Hinges & Door Locks. Every six months, grease all hinges and latches including doors, trunk, hood, gas cap door, door locks, and ignition. Use white lithium grease for most applications. Use graphite lubricant for locks and ignition. WD-40 is light-duty oil and will work for everything, possibly just not as long. WD-40 is especially good for anything with rust. If you experience problems with your ignition, see page 37 for possible solutions.

Important: Use your key (instead of your remote) to open the driver and passenger doors on occasion. Over time, debris gets into the door lock and may prevent your key from working. This could be a problem if the remote is lost or if the battery stops working. Oil the locks and use the key to keep everything working smoothly.

Lights & Blinkers. At least once a month, check the front and back lights of the car. It is fast and easy to have someone walk to the front and rear of the vehicle as you test all of your lights, or you can check the lights by yourself.

To check the lights by yourself: at night, pull up to any wall, fence, front of a store, etc. Check headlights, high and low beams. Check your left blinker, then right blinker, then the back lights.

Back up to a wall, fence, store, etc. While using your rearview and/or side mirrors, step on the brake to make sure brake lights are working. Check both blinkers. Turn headlights off and on to make sure tail lights are working. Put car in reverse (with foot firmly on the brake) to check the backup lights. Also check your license plate light. Police can issue tickets for any non-working lights on your car.

Parking/Emergency Brake. The emergency brake should be used every time you park. It keeps weight off of the transmission and therefore makes your transmission last longer. Especially if parking any place other than on totally flat ground, that brake should be used. Releasing the brake when you start to drive is also very important. Driving with the emergency brake engaged can cause damage to the cable and also to your regular brakes.

The emergency brake cable is encased in a protective sleeve but if not used frequently, the cable can become corroded and rusted and can fail to work.

How to use the emergency brake in an emergency: If your brakes were to ever go out, the emergency brake can save your life; HOW-EVER, you must remain calm and slowly pull up the lever or slowly push down the pedal (whichever your car has). This will help slow your car and allow you to bring it to a more controlled stop.

Applying the emergency brake quickly will cause the car to fishtail, lock up or skid, and you will lose control of the car. Never turn off your car because the power steering will not work.

Timing Belt/Chain. Most vehicles have either a timing belt or timing chain. If the car has a timing belt, that belt will need to be replaced at the manufacturer's recommended time. If the belt breaks, the engine can be damaged or ruined.

Some vehicles have a timing *chain*, which tends to last much longer than a belt and, depending on the vehicle, may never need replacing. Know whether your vehicle has a timing belt or chain, and know when service is needed. This is an expensive repair because the engine must be mostly dismantled and reassembled (*lots* of labor time) to replace a belt that costs around $20.

Tires. Worn tires and over/under inflated tires can be hazardous on wet roads. Tires that wear unevenly can also indicate alignment problems. If your car runs rough on some roads, your tires might need to be rotated or balanced. Tires generally should be rotated about every 5,000 - 7,500 miles.

Tires have "wear marks" that show when the tread is getting low; ask your tire store to show you how this looks or Google it. Tires can also be checked by inserting a penny into the tread (Lincoln should be upside down). If you can see the top of Lincoln's head, your tread is too worn and it is time to buy new tires.

Tire Pressure. Keep a good quality tire gauge in your car, and learn how to use it. There should be a sticker inside the driver's door frame that shows how much air your tires need. That information is also in the Owner's Manual.

If tires are under- or over-inflated, they will wear unevenly and you will need new tires more quickly. Improper air pressure is unsafe, especially in rain or other bad road conditions. Also, it will decrease your gas mileage.

Tire pressure should be checked at least once each month, although checking with each gasoline fill-up is actually advised by experts. For the most accurate reading, check tires when they are cold. Remember to also check the air in the spare tire. *Note: If your spare tire is a "doughnut," it is designed for emergency use and is not reliable for extended driving.*

Weather-stripping. Rubber strips around doors and windows (weather-stripping) should be lubricated every six months for best wear. To keep weather-stripping from drying out and cracking, use a product like ArmorAll that is made to condition and protect rubber.

Tips for Buying a Used Car

• When buying a vehicle newer than you currently own, your car insurance may increase. In states with an annual tag fee, that fee will also increase. If you are on a tight budget, it might be worthwhile to find out how much those items will cost before buying the new car.

• Do your homework. There are multiple sites where you can research every type of vehicle. Read both positive and negative comments, but pay close attention to the negative ones. You might want to avoid manufacturing years that had the most problems.

> *Save yourself a lot of money and headache by doing a little research before buying.*

• When buying from a dealership, shop the *"certified"* used/pre-owned vehicles with confidence. This means extended warranties are available, backed by the original vehicle manufacturer. The vehicle should have received a 100-point inspection and any problems found were fixed. If big problems are found, the vehicle will be disqualified from the certified program.

• Dealerships and other used car businesses may offer third party warranties on select used vehicles. Find out the cost of this warranty – and all other fees, taxes, etc. UP FRONT (they usually wait until they are closing the deal). If you want the security of a warranty AND to know exactly what your payment will be, do not wait until the deal is closing. You might discover your monthly payment will be higher than you thought (or can afford).

• A CARFAX report will tell you if the car has been in accidents, leased, and may list warranty work done; however, it really does not tell as much as one would think. Google "what does CARFAX leave out." Try to get the car dealer or private owner to provide that report instead of spending $30+ to get a report on each car you're interested in. By the way, the CARFAX report is a good selling tool for private owners. People are used to asking for it.

There are CARFAX reports you can get for free. In your browser, type: http://www.carfax.com/free carfax reports.cfx. Scroll to the bottom of that page to "Free Services." Free reports you can access include Lemon Check, Record Check, Recall Check, and Problem Car Check.

For those who don't know, there is a "Lemon Law" that protects consumers when cars are just not made well. For more information, go to: www.lemonlawamerica.com.

- Where was the car manufactured and where has it been driven? If it comes from an area that has experienced flooding or other disasters, don't buy it. If the car has been driven in the North (where salt and other chemicals are used to de-ice roads in the winter), have it checked out by a good mechanic. There could be substantial rust on the undercarriage, throughout the motor, on the wheels, etc.

- Even if the seller promises the oil, brakes and fluids are new, have everything checked. Mechanics recommend getting new oil, brakes and fluids, just so you will know everything is in good shape.

- Find out (Google it) if that particular vehicle requires a timing belt or any other expensive service that might be due or overdue. Timing belts are frequently very expensive to replace (can be up to $1,000), and your entire engine can be ruined if that belt breaks. If the car you like has a timing belt, ask if the belt has been replaced. The seller must have the paperwork confirming that repair. If they don't know what that is or have not replaced it, make the replacement cost part of your negotiations if you still want that car.

- When buying a used car from a private owner or independent used car dealer, call a dealership to see if they do pre-purchase inspections. If they do, it could be free or up to $150. Call before going; you might need an appointment. They will check everything possible, and you will have a better idea of the car's true condition. However, understand that things can go wrong even if the car passes all of the tests. Things can be missed by mechanics and computerized machines.

If the seller will not agree to let you have the car inspected, you should probably be suspicious of buying that car.

• Whether buying from a dealer or private seller, always ask why the car is being sold, was traded, etc. The salesman/dealer might not know, but always ask. Also ask if it would be possible to talk with the previous owner. Sometimes that is an option.

If a private seller tells you a story that does not sound quite right, it might be wise to consider other cars.

• Always take someone with you to buy a car. Two sets of eyes are better than one. The other person is not emotionally connected to buying a car and should be able to see things from a more unbiased viewpoint. Hopefully, that person will be able to point out helpful things you might miss.

• If you don't feel some level of trust with the salesman or private owner, or if you have a bad "gut feeling" about the situation, it is usually best to not buy what they are selling. It is also good to feel comfortable about the area of town where you are shopping.

• Try not to get caught in a "need it today" situation – and never express desperation. Sellers might raise the price if they know you are hooked. Also, never say how much you "love, love, love" the car! Keep a poker face (stay cool) and negotiate your best deal. It is always good to say something like, "We are looking at several possibilities right now. What is the best price you can give me?" That is a respectful way to give the seller an opportunity to lower his price.

• If your vehicle mileage is high and/or your repair bills are becoming more frequent and expensive, or if your mechanic says your car is likely to experience big repairs in the future, it might be time to think about selling or trading in your car.

Most of us don't want to sell our problems to someone else (unless we are totally honest about what is wrong and price the car accordingly). If that's the case, ask your mechanic if he wants to buy it.

Some mechanics are interested in buying a car they know and can fix, or he might know someone who would want it. Don't just give it away – know what it is worth.

If you do not sell your car outright, it can be beneficial to trade it in on another used car – but not always. Do your research and find the best deal for you.

- What is the car worth? The most commonly used websites are: www.kbb.com (Kelly Blue Book) and www.nada.com. Banks generally use Kelly Blue Book for the amount they will *loan* on a car. NADA will give you a better idea of the actual value of the car.

- Most people do not carry cash when they are shopping for a vehicle; however, they will have cash when they return to make the purchase. People have been killed for small amounts of money. Carrying thousands of dollars in cash can make you a very attractive target. Instead of carrying cash, purchasing a Cashier's Check from your bank could be a better option.

Even better: When meeting with a private seller, the best plan is to meet at your bank and make the cash withdrawal or get a Cashier's Check while the seller is with you inside the bank.

If the seller refuses to meet you at a safe public place, you should not take the chance of getting into a dangerous situation where you could be robbed or worse.

- Pre-arranging financing with a bank or credit union instead of financing through a dealership may give you better interest rates.

Buyer Checklist

- Never buy a car you have only seen in the dark. Too many things can be missed that would be easily seen in daylight.

- Exterior: check for rust spots/dents; use a magnet to identify places where plastic fillers or resin were used for repairs. Be sure vehicle sets level, hood is level with the car, no obvious signs of body damage, and that tires are wearing evening and show no signs of dry-rot cracking. Try all door handles, inside and out.

- Interior: check for wet spots, mold; CD player/radio works; heating & cooling systems work properly

- Before starting vehicle, make sure all dash lights work: the check engine light, air bags light, battery light, etc.

- Trunk/back area: check for rust, holes, cracks, and mold (can indicate water seepage), also spare tire and tire jack

- Radiator: hoses should be firm and sturdy, not soft or cracked. Remove radiator cap: brown or dirty coolant may indicate head gasket leak

- How clean is the oil? Are the other fluid levels full?

- Timing belt or chain: important information to know

- Transmission: fluid should be red or pink, no burnt smell

- Engine Block: dark oil stains can indicate leak in the gasket

- If possible, take vehicle to mechanic or dealership to be checked out more thoroughly

Regardless of how careful you are, it is easy to miss something when you are trying to see everything – a good reason to take along a friend. Realize that used cars frequently need some work. The object is to try to catch any major, more expensive problems.

Batteries & Jumper Cables

Battery Basics

Starting an engine requires a lot of power from the battery. After starting the engine, a car must run about 30 minutes for the battery to recharge. Short trips (or starting and turning off your car several times) weaken and discharge the battery. In that case, a weak battery may not be able to recharge without driving the vehicle.

If your car is not used regularly, start the car at least once a week and let it run for 30 minutes. When a car is not being driven, there is usually a slight drain on the battery. That adds up over time and not only drains the battery but can ruin it.

When the Battery is not Charging

Vehicles have a gauge or "trouble light" that shows if the battery is charging. If the trouble light is on or if the gauge shows to the left (negative) side of the mark, the engine is draining power from the battery. The battery light may indicate alternator problems.

If the battery is being drained, turn off the A/C and radio. If it is daytime, turn off the headlights. Then get to a safe place: home, mechanic, or auto parts store because your engine may quit. Do not turn your car off until you are where you want to be; it may not start again with that battery.

Jumper cables or a Jump Box may offer a temporary solution; however, the battery may need to be replaced and a new alternator might be needed. Dealerships, mechanics, or auto parts stores can check your battery to see if it needs to be replaced. Always keep receipts for batteries. If the battery fails prior to the expiration date, you will get credit toward a replacement battery.

Battery Terminals

The terminals are short posts on the top of the battery; the battery cables are connected to them. You might see white, powdery residue on or around the terminals. This is called corrosion and is the same powder you see if batteries are left in a flashlight too long. The corrosion will eventually keep your battery from getting power (current).

To clean the terminals, put a tablespoon of baking soda on each terminal and pour a small amount of water on it. It will sizzle. Take an old toothbrush and scrub around the terminals. Use more water to wash the baking soda and corrosion off the battery. Wash your hands well with soap and water when you finish.

If a corroded battery leaves you stranded, you can pour dark cola on the terminals. It should eat away enough corrosion to get the engine started again; however, jumper cables may be needed because the battery could have been worn down while trying to start it.

Auto Supply stores sell a protective sealer spray that can be applied to clean battery terminals; they also sell a cleaner, but you can use baking soda to do that. The sealer (around $5) will prevent corrosion from building up on the terminals.

How to Use Jumper Cables
Before you attach the cables:
- Pull the running car (car #1) close to where the battery is located in car #2.
- Unplug any electronics – cell phones, iPods, etc., and turn off radio and all lights.
- Turn car #1 off and open the hoods of both cars.
- Pull cables out straight. Do not let the positive and negative ends touch.

Attaching the cables:
(1) Terminals are marked with a + or – sign. Attach the positive (+) cable (red wire or handle) to the (+) battery terminal in car #1.
(2) Connect other end of the red wire to the positive (+) terminal in car #2.
(3) Attach negative (–) cable (black wire or handle) to the (–) battery terminal in car #1.
(4) In car #2, attach the other black-handled wire to some metal if possible (like a motor mount or metal battery bracket). If there is no metal, attach to the negative terminal in car #2. There could be sparks when this connection is made.

(5) Start car #1; run it about five minutes (with the jumper cables connected) before starting car #2. Run car #1 at fast idle while other person starts car #2.

If the battery is dead because lights were left on, it should only take a few minutes before car #2 starts. If car #2 does not start, let it continue receiving the battery charge for about 10 minutes. If it doesn't start after three or four tries, do NOT continue trying. You may flood the engine and could damage the starter. Call a tow truck.

Removing the cables:

To remove cables, reverse the above instructions. Remove black cable (-) from car #2, then from car #1. Remove red cable (+) from car #2, then from car #1.

While this seems a simple procedure, it can be dangerous. If possible, wear eye protection and never smoke when close to the battery.

Refer to Owner's Manual for exact instructions for your vehicle.

NOTE: Some people prefer to turn off car #1 after giving jump to car #2, then disconnect cables before car #2 tries to start. This can protect the alternator.

Using a Jump Box

For older or rarely used vehicles that might need a jump more often, a Jump Box could be a good investment. Plug box into an electrical outlet to charge it, then keep it in your car. The Jump Box will lose its charge over time, so it must be recharged periodically. The Jump Box owner's manual should indicate how long it holds a charge and proper usage.

When purchasing a Jump Box, a smaller model is fine for a small car, but higher amperage is needed for larger vehicles like vans, SUVs and trucks.

Leading & Following

At some point, everyone will either lead or follow another car. This can be stressful as the lead car changes lanes and leaves the follower car in a panic as they frantically try to regain position behind the lead car. Although having a GPS might make following another car less troublesome for some, there are always situations where it is good to know how to lead and follow.

The following technique is guaranteed to reduce stress and increase safety, especially on multi-lane roads:

- When the lead car (Car #1) needs to change lanes, he signals (uses blinker) and <u>waits</u> until the second car (Car #2) acknowledges (uses blinker), then Car #2 changes lanes. *Car #1 has not changed lanes at this point.*

- Once Car #2 has safely changed lanes, he leaves space for Car #1 to move into position in front of him. Car #1 signals and safely moves in front of Car #2.

- If there are three cars, Car #1 signals, then Car #2 signals to Car #3. The first two cars wait until Car #3 can safely change lanes – thereby clearing a space for the two cars in front to safely move over.

- When another car is following you, travel at a speed that is comfortable for the other driver(s).

If you get separated:

Car #1 must watch traffic lights and not leave Car #2 (or #3) if possible. If Car #1 gets separated, he should safely pull off the road and wait for the other car(s) to catch up.

As Car #2 approaches, he slows down to leave space for Car #1 to safely pull back into traffic and resume the lead.

Be sure to watch the traffic behind as you slow down and, if necessary, pump your brakes to signal you are slowing your speed.

Brake pumping (two or three short pumps) should alert the follower cars that something is going on. (Decide on that signal with the other drivers before starting your trip.)

When following on a road with stop signs, the lead driver should make prior arrangements with the follower cars that if they get separated, the lead driver will pull off and wait. This will eliminate additional stress for the follower drivers.

Most important: give each driver the address and general description of where you are going, landmarks, etc., if possible. Also, make sure each driver has the cell phone numbers of the other drivers.

Driving & More

Thank you for your interest in this book! Hopefully, you have learned new, useful information and to be a safer, more aware driver. This book was written to provide safety advice and general car knowledge. In no way is it meant to be *THE* ultimate book of all car safety and repair facts! Always refer to your Owner's Manual and certified mechanics for information specific to your vehicle.

In closing, I wanted to leave you with some basic good advice. While these points can be related to driving, they may also help you look at some things differently and could possibly impact other aspects of your life.

• Regardless of the question (cars, health, happiness, cooking, gardening, etc.), always look up the answer for yourself. It is easy to do with the Internet. Well-meaning people, including friends and professionals, sometimes have a problem saying "I don't know." Instead, they will give you their opinion, best guess, or what they believe to be true – but will present it as fact. Always check the facts for yourself and especially for important questions, check your facts with more than one source.

• The definition of insanity is *continuing to do the same thing over and over while expecting a different result.* Regardless of what we want to change, we have to do something different to make it happen.

• Focus on positive thoughts instead of negative ones/problems. Focusing on problems does nothing except add to our frustration. Instead, think about possible solutions and how the problem can be turned around.

• Nobody is perfect – not parents, bosses, friends or strangers, and we as individuals are not perfect either! To keep peace and positive energy in our lives, we must be willing to give everyone else the same consideration and respect we want them to give us.

"If we did all the things we are capable of doing, we would literally astound ourselves."
- Thomas A. Edison

Notes

Notes

Notes

SERVICE RECORD

DATE	MILEAGE	ITEM OR SERVICE	COST

SERVICE RECORD

DATE	MILEAGE	ITEM OR SERVICE	COST

SERVICE RECORD

DATE	MILEAGE	ITEM OR SERVICE	COST

SERVICE RECORD

DATE	MILEAGE	ITEM OR SERVICE	COST

SERVICE RECORD

DATE	MILEAGE	ITEM OR SERVICE	COST

SERVICE RECORD

DATE	MILEAGE	ITEM OR SERVICE	COST

SERVICE RECORD

DATE	MILEAGE	ITEM OR SERVICE	COST

SERVICE RECORD

DATE	MILEAGE	ITEM OR SERVICE	COST

BASIC MAINTENANCE CHECKLIST

YEAR _____

	JAN	FEB	MAR	APR	MAY	JUN	JUL	AUG	SEP	OCT	NOV	DEC
Alignment												
Antifreeze/Coolant (radiator)												
Battery												
Brakes												
Brake Fluid												
Hinges & Locks												
Lights & Blinkers												
Oil												
Power Steering Fluid												
Tires & Tire Pressure												
Transmission Fluid												
Weather Stripping												

NOTES: _____

BASIC MAINTENANCE CHECKLIST

YEAR _____

	JAN	FEB	MAR	APR	MAY	JUN	JUL	AUG	SEP	OCT	NOV	DEC
Alignment												
Antifreeze/Coolant (radiator)												
Battery												
Brakes												
Brake Fluid												
Hinges & Locks												
Lights & Blinkers												
Oil												
Power Steering Fluid												
Tires & Tire Pressure												
Transmission Fluid												
Weather Stripping												

NOTES: _____

BASIC MAINTENANCE CHECKLIST

YEAR _____

	JAN	FEB	MAR	APR	MAY	JUN	JUL	AUG	SEP	OCT	NOV	DEC
Alignment												
Antifreeze/Coolant (radiator)												
Battery												
Brakes												
Brake Fluid												
Hinges & Locks												
Lights & Blinkers												
Oil												
Power Steering Fluid												
Tires & Tire Pressure												
Transmission Fluid												
Weather Stripping												

NOTES: _____

BASIC MAINTENANCE CHECKLIST

YEAR _____

	JAN	FEB	MAR	APR	MAY	JUN	JUL	AUG	SEP	OCT	NOV	DEC
Alignment												
Antifreeze/Coolant (radiator)												
Battery												
Brakes												
Brake Fluid												
Hinges & Locks												
Lights & Blinkers												
Oil												
Power Steering Fluid												
Tires & Tire Pressure												
Transmission Fluid												
Weather Stripping												

NOTES: _____

_____

_____

BASIC MAINTENANCE CHECKLIST

YEAR _____

	JAN	FEB	MAR	APR	MAY	JUN	JUL	AUG	SEP	OCT	NOV	DEC
Alignment												
Antifreeze/Coolant (radiator)												
Battery												
Brakes												
Brake Fluid												
Hinges & Locks												
Lights & Blinkers												
Oil												
Power Steering Fluid												
Tires & Tire Pressure												
Transmission Fluid												
Weather Stripping												

NOTES: _____

_____

BASIC MAINTENANCE CHECKLIST

YEAR _____

	JAN	FEB	MAR	APR	MAY	JUN	JUL	AUG	SEP	OCT	NOV	DEC
Alignment												
Antifreeze/Coolant (radiator)												
Battery												
Brakes												
Brake Fluid												
Hinges & Locks												
Lights & Blinkers												
Oil												
Power Steering Fluid												
Tires & Tire Pressure												
Transmission Fluid												
Weather Stripping												

NOTES: _____

BASIC MAINTENANCE CHECKLIST

YEAR _____

	JAN	FEB	MAR	APR	MAY	JUN	JUL	AUG	SEP	OCT	NOV	DEC
Alignment												
Antifreeze/Coolant (radiator)												
Battery												
Brakes												
Brake Fluid												
Hinges & Locks												
Lights & Blinkers												
Oil												
Power Steering Fluid												
Tires & Tire Pressure												
Transmission Fluid												
Weather Stripping												

NOTES: _____

Index

www.ingramcontent.com/pod-product-compliance
Lightning Source LLC
Chambersburg PA
CBHW071339290326
41933CB00040B/1823